MARY COMPANY

NEW CAREER

Copyright © 2024 by Mary Company

All rights reserved. No part of this publication may be reproduced, stored or transmitted in any form or by any means, electronic, mechanical, photocopying, recording, scanning, or otherwise without written permission from the publisher. It is illegal to copy this book, post it to a website, or distribute it by any other means without permission.

First edition

This book was professionally typeset on Reedsy.
Find out more at reedsy.com

This book is dedicated to God Almighty

Contents

Preface		ii
Acknowledgments		iv
1	The Turning Point	1
2	Exploring Passions	4
3	Navigating the Unknown	8
4	Embracing Challenges	12
5	New Connections	17
6	The Art of Letting Go	21
7	Embracing Vulnerability	25
8	A New Chapter Begins	29
9	Embracing Challenges	34
10	A New Direction	39
11	The Collective Exhibition	44
12	New Beginnings	48
About the Author		52

Preface

In New Career, we follow the inspiring journey of Clara Evans, a woman in her late 40s who courageously decides to shift her career from a mundane corporate job to a fulfilling path in art therapy. Struggling with the weight of unfulfilled dreams and a longing for purpose, Clara takes a leap of faith after a life-altering moment pushes her to reevaluate her life choices.

As she embarks on this transformative journey, Clara faces the daunting challenges of starting anew in a field that is both rewarding and emotionally demanding. She navigates the complexities of her new role, learning to connect with individuals struggling with mental health issues through the healing power of art. Along the way, she encounters a diverse group of participants, each with their own unique stories, struggles, and triumphs.

With the support of newfound friends and mentors, Clara creates workshops that provide safe spaces for self-expression and healing. Her passion ignites a spark within her community, leading to increased interest and collaboration from local organizations. However, she also confronts her own insecurities and fears of inadequacy, grappling with the question of whether she truly belongs in this new world.

Through personal growth, vulnerability, and resilience, Clara discovers not only her own potential but also the profound impact of her work on the lives of others. Her journey is further highlighted by a surprise radio interview that brings her mission into the spotlight, leading to new opportunities and challenges.

As Clara learns to embrace change and harness her creativity, she becomes a beacon of hope and inspiration, proving that it is never too late to pursue one's dreams and make a difference. In a powerful conclusion, she reflects on the importance of community, the beauty of artistic expression, and the strength that comes from sharing one's story.

New Career is a heartfelt narrative that celebrates the transformative power of art, the courage to embrace new beginnings, and the enduring spirit of those who strive to make the world a better place, one brushstroke at a time.

Acknowledgments

Thank you for your love and support

1

The Turning Point

Clara Thompson sat in her modest office cubicle, staring blankly at the rows of spreadsheets on her computer screen. The fluorescent lights hummed above her, casting a sterile glow over the beige walls that felt as confining as the corporate culture that surrounded her. At 48, she had been climbing the corporate ladder for nearly two decades, yet she felt as if she had reached a plateau. The thrill of meetings, presentations, and deadlines had long faded, leaving behind a gnawing sense of discontent.

Her phone buzzed with a reminder for a conference call with her team, but Clara couldn't muster the energy to care. The usual small talk about quarterly results and departmental goals felt monotonous and devoid of purpose. As she pressed the mute button, she caught a glimpse of her reflection in the glass window beside her. Tired eyes stared back, framed by a pair of glasses that had become more of a necessity than a style choice. It was a stark reminder of the years spent in a job that no longer ignited her passion.

The conference call droned on in the background, but Clara's thoughts wandered to her life outside of work. She had once been vibrant, filled with dreams and ambitions, but somewhere along the way, she had lost herself. The years spent raising her children, navigating a rocky marriage, and dedicating herself to her career had taken their toll. With her kids now adults and living independently, she felt a void—a sense that life had passed her by while she was busy ticking boxes on someone else's agenda.

It was during one of her quiet lunches, a solitary salad from the cafeteria, that the turning point arrived. Clara overheard a conversation at the next table between two younger colleagues. They were discussing their aspirations, their travels, and their hopes for the future. They spoke with an enthusiasm that Clara realized she hadn't felt in years. A wave of nostalgia washed over her as she remembered her own dreams—writing, painting, traveling the world. She had pushed those aspirations aside, convinced that practicality and stability were more important than following her heart.

That evening, as Clara returned home to her small but cozy apartment, she sat on the couch with a journal and a pen, something she hadn't done in years. The pages were blank, waiting for her thoughts to spill out. She wrote about her day, her frustrations at work, and the conversation that had sparked something inside her. As the words flowed, she felt a flicker of excitement. Perhaps it was time to reevaluate her life choices, to consider what it would mean to chase after those long-forgotten dreams.

Days turned into weeks, and Clara found herself increasingly distracted at work. Each email reminder of deadlines became a nudge towards introspection. She began to research career options outside her current role. Could she turn her love for writing into a career? Maybe a job in education, where she could inspire others, would bring her joy. The more she explored, the more she realized how much she had stifled her own aspirations in favor of a comfortable routine.

One evening, as she prepared dinner, she found herself lost in thought about the future. The kitchen filled with the aroma of sautéed vegetables, but all she could think about was her potential new life. She remembered her grandmother, who had taken a leap of faith in her late forties, leaving her small town to pursue a career in nursing. Clara often recalled the way her grandmother spoke about her decision with pride. It had transformed her life, and Clara wondered if she too could make such a bold move.

That weekend, Clara attended a local workshop on career transitions, a gathering of people at various stages of their lives looking for change. Surrounded by others who shared her desire for reinvention, Clara felt a sense of camaraderie. They exchanged stories, laughed, and encouraged one another. For the first time in years, Clara felt a sense of hope. Maybe, just maybe, she could step away from the corporate grind and embark on a new journey.

The following Monday, as she walked into the office, Clara was filled with determination. She resolved to make a change, to embrace the possibility of a new career. The familiar hum of the office now felt different; it was a backdrop to her realization that she was on the brink of something transformative. Clara knew the road ahead would be challenging, but for the first time in years, she felt ready to take that leap. The spark had been ignited, and she was determined to fan the flames of her newfound ambition.

2

Exploring Passions

Clara woke up the next morning feeling a sense of urgency coursing through her veins. It was as if the very air around her vibrated with possibilities. The sun streamed through her bedroom window, casting warm rays that danced across her walls, igniting a sense of hope and renewal. Today, she promised herself, she would begin to explore the passions she had long neglected.

After a quick breakfast, Clara made her way to her small desk, cluttered with papers and mementos from her past. She pushed aside the old files from her corporate days and opened her laptop. The first thing she did was pull up a blank document. Staring at the blinking cursor, she felt a mix of excitement and trepidation. What would she write? What passions had she buried so deep that they felt like whispers in her heart?

Clara decided to start with a list. She took a deep breath and typed, "Things I Love." As the words flowed, she felt lighter with each entry.

1. **Writing** - Ever since she was a child, Clara had been captivated by the written word. She remembered losing herself in novels, the way characters came alive and transported her to different worlds. It was her escape, her therapy.

2. **Painting** - During her college years, Clara had dabbled in painting, experimenting with colors and canvases. The sensation of the brush gliding across the surface was exhilarating, but she had stopped after graduation, believing it was impractical to pursue as a career.

3. **Traveling** - Clara longed to explore new cultures, to immerse herself in different ways of life. She had visited a few countries in her twenties, but responsibilities had kept her from venturing out in recent years.

4. **Cooking** - While cooking had started as a necessity, it transformed into a passion. Clara found joy in creating meals, experimenting with recipes, and sharing food with family and friends.

5. **Teaching** - Clara remembered the joy she felt when she helped her children with their homework. The satisfaction of sharing knowledge and seeing someone else grow was fulfilling.

As she typed her list, Clara began to realize that each of these passions intertwined with her life story, reflecting parts of her that had been silenced for too long. With her heart racing, she thought about how to incorporate them into a new career.

The idea of writing struck a chord with her. Clara had always dreamed of becoming a writer, but life had taken her on a different path. Could she still pursue this passion? She opened a new tab and searched for writing courses. As she scrolled through various options, her excitement grew. She found a local community college offering a creative writing program, along with online courses that focused on blogging and storytelling.

"Why not both?" Clara mused to herself, jotting down the information. The thought of meeting like-minded individuals who shared her love for writing filled her with anticipation.

Next, she thought about painting. Perhaps she could take an art class to reignite that creative spark. There was a studio nearby that offered weekend workshops for beginners and seasoned artists alike. She made a note to check their schedule later.

As she explored these passions, Clara felt a surge of energy she hadn't felt in years. The notion of combining her love for writing and cooking also emerged. Maybe she could start a food blog, sharing her culinary adventures and recipes with others. The thought excited her—cooking was not just about sustenance; it was an art form, an expression of love and creativity.

But before diving headfirst into her newfound aspirations, Clara knew she needed to gain some clarity on her goals. That evening, she set aside time for introspection. Armed with her journal, she sat on the couch, a warm cup of herbal tea in hand, and reflected on what she truly wanted.

She wrote about her dreams, fears, and desires. **What if I fail?** flashed through her mind, but she quickly countered it with, **What if I succeed?** Each stroke of her pen felt liberating. Clara began to formulate a plan, envisioning a roadmap that would lead her to explore her passions further.

The next morning, Clara decided to sign up for the creative writing course. It felt like a significant step toward reclaiming her identity. She was both nervous and thrilled, contemplating how to juggle her current job while embarking on this new journey. But deep down, she knew that taking these steps was essential to her growth.

Over the following weeks, Clara plunged into her writing class with enthusiasm. The instructor encouraged her to embrace her voice, reminding her that there were no wrong answers when it came to self-expression. She found herself writing poetry, short stories, and even a few reflective essays about her life. Each word penned down felt like a step toward liberation.

Outside of writing, Clara attended the painting workshop she had discovered. The first day was intimidating—she stood alongside young artists, all seemingly more skilled than she was. But as she picked up the brush and allowed herself to be swept away by the colors, she realized that this was not about comparison; it was about reconnecting with herself.

Gradually, Clara felt like the woman she used to be, the one who lived with passion and purpose. The writing and painting provided an outlet for her emotions and allowed her to explore her creativity.

With each passing day, Clara was transforming. The void she had felt for so long began to fill with color, inspiration, and the promise of a future that was entirely her own. As she walked home one evening, she looked up at the sky, marveling at the beauty around her. For the first time in years, Clara felt alive, ready to embrace whatever came next in her journey of self-discovery.

3

Navigating the Unknown

With the arrival of spring, Clara found herself awakening each morning with a renewed sense of purpose. The days were longer, and the sun shone brighter, echoing the transformation taking place within her. She immersed herself in her creative writing and painting classes, finding joy in the process of discovery. Yet, as the initial excitement began to settle, Clara realized she needed to confront the reality of what her career shift would entail.

During one particularly enlightening writing class, her instructor, Mr. Carter, encouraged students to share their stories. Each participant took turns reading their work, revealing personal anecdotes that resonated deeply within the room. Clara listened intently, absorbing the raw emotions and diverse experiences. When it was her turn, her heart raced.

She chose to read a piece about her journey—the struggles of finding herself after years of dedication to a career that had drained her spirit. As she spoke, Clara felt a catharsis wash over her. The vulnerability in sharing her story sparked an unexpected connection with her classmates. At the end of the session, several students approached her, offering their support and sharing similar experiences.

"Thank you for your honesty, Clara," a young woman named Mia said. "I'm also trying to figure out my next steps, and hearing your story makes me feel less alone."

This sense of community was invaluable to Clara. In those moments, she understood that her journey was not just about her; it was a shared human experience. The collective pursuit of passion and fulfillment resonated deeply, giving her the courage to embrace the unknown.

However, Clara also recognized that stepping away from her corporate job would not be easy. The reality of financial stability loomed over her thoughts like a shadow. After weeks of intense introspection, she decided it was time to take a practical approach to her newfound passions. She would need to create a solid plan—one that balanced her creative pursuits with her financial responsibilities.

That Saturday, Clara sat at her kitchen table, papers strewn around her like colorful leaves in autumn. She grabbed her notebook and a pen, jotting down her thoughts.

1. Assessing Financial Needs
   She calculated her monthly expenses—rent, utilities, groceries, and a few occasional luxuries like yoga classes or dining out. The figure felt daunting, but Clara reassured herself that she could make adjustments if necessary. She could reduce her spending by cooking more at home and limiting unnecessary expenses.

2. Creating a Timeline
   Clara set a timeline for her career transition. She decided to remain in her corporate job for another six months, during which she would continue her writing and painting classes, gradually building her portfolio. At the same time, she could explore opportunities for freelance writing or part-time work in fields related to her passions.

3. Networking and Building Connections

Understanding the importance of networking, Clara made a note to attend local art exhibitions, writers' workshops, and community events. She realized that building connections in her desired fields would open doors and provide invaluable insights.

4. Embracing the Journey

Finally, she reminded herself to enjoy the process. This journey wasn't merely about the destination; it was about rediscovering who she was. She wanted to celebrate the small victories along the way, savoring the moments of creativity and connection.

Feeling satisfied with her plan, Clara took a deep breath, releasing the tension that had built up inside her. She was ready to navigate the unknown, fueled by determination and a sense of adventure.

In the following weeks, Clara diligently worked on her writing and painting, honing her skills and experimenting with different styles. She began posting her artwork and short stories on social media, creating a small online presence that allowed her to connect with other artists and writers. The feedback she received was encouraging, igniting a fire within her that she hadn't felt in years.

One evening, while perusing a local community center's website, Clara stumbled upon an announcement for a small art exhibit showcasing local artists. An idea sparked in her mind: what if she submitted her paintings? The thought made her heart race. Clara hesitated, grappling with the familiar wave of self-doubt that had often held her back.

"What if they don't like my work?" she whispered to herself, but the voice of encouragement that had grown within her responded, "What if they do?"

Taking a deep breath, she decided to submit two pieces—an abstract painting that represented her journey of transformation and another inspired by a serene landscape she had painted during a weekend retreat. The submission process required a short artist statement, and as she penned her thoughts, Clara realized that sharing her journey through art would be a powerful way to connect with others.

Weeks later, the day of the exhibit arrived, and Clara felt a mixture of excitement and nerves. She arrived at the community center early to set up her work. As she hung her paintings on the wall, Clara felt a rush of pride. This was her first step into the art world, and she was ready to share her story.

As guests arrived, Clara mingled, engaging in conversations that filled the air with energy. People complimented her work, and the discussions flowed effortlessly. She found herself sharing the stories behind her paintings, speaking with passion about her journey and how each piece represented a facet of her evolving identity.

In those moments, Clara felt alive—connected to her art and to the people who appreciated it. The fears that had once held her back began to fade as she embraced her newfound identity as an artist and writer. It was a reminder that the unknown, while daunting, could also be exhilarating.

That night, as she returned home, Clara reflected on how far she had come in such a short time. She had begun to navigate her journey into a new career, fueled by passion, purpose, and the unwavering belief that it was never too late to rewrite her story. With each step, she was learning to trust herself, and the unknown felt less intimidating and more like an adventure waiting to unfold.

4

Embracing Challenges

As spring blossomed into summer, Clara's days became filled with a whirlwind of activities, both creative and practical. The excitement of her newfound passions propelled her forward, but with that enthusiasm came the realization that change was not without its hurdles. The delicate balance between her corporate job and her artistic pursuits often felt precarious, and Clara found herself at a crossroads that tested her resolve.

One afternoon, Clara sat at her kitchen table, the familiar clutter of papers and art supplies surrounding her. She had just returned from work, where the pressures of deadlines and meetings had worn her thin. Although she loved her job, the daily grind had become increasingly exhausting, leaving little room for her passions. She gazed out the window, watching the sun set in a vibrant blaze of colors—a stunning display that reminded her of the art she was striving to create.

Clara sighed, knowing she had to make a decision soon. The creative writing and painting classes were invigorating, but they also demanded time and focus. The deadlines for her upcoming art exhibit were approaching, and she felt the weight of her commitments pressing down on her shoulders. As she contemplated her next steps, she realized she needed to have a serious conversation with herself about her priorities.

After a brief break, Clara opened her laptop and began to write a letter to herself, a practice she found immensely helpful. As she typed, she poured her thoughts onto the page:

Dear Clara,

I know you're feeling overwhelmed right now. The truth is, you're trying to juggle a lot—your corporate job, your writing, your painting, and your family responsibilities. It's a lot for anyone, but especially for someone embarking on such a transformative journey.

Remember why you started this. You wanted to rediscover your passions, to reclaim the parts of yourself that you let slip away over the years. You deserve to pursue what makes you happy, but it's okay to acknowledge that it won't always be easy.

Consider your options carefully. Can you streamline your responsibilities at work? Can you find a way to allocate specific times for your creative endeavors without compromising your current job? Perhaps you could even look into transitioning to a part-time role in your company. It's okay to take a leap of faith—life is too short to not chase your dreams.

Don't forget to breathe. Take things one step at a time. You're on a path of growth, and every challenge you face is a chance to learn.

With her heart a little lighter, Clara closed her laptop and took a deep breath. The next morning, she resolved to speak to her manager about potentially shifting her workload. She felt a mix of anxiety and excitement as she headed into the office. The thought of broaching the subject filled her with trepidation; what if her manager didn't understand? What if she was seen as uncommitted? But the desire to follow her passions outweighed her fears.

Later that day, Clara found a moment to talk to Greg, her manager. "Hey, Greg, do you have a minute?" she asked, her voice steady despite the nervous flutter in her stomach.

"Sure, Clara! What's up?" he replied, looking up from his desk with a friendly smile.

"I've been reflecting on my workload lately," Clara began, gathering her thoughts. "I love my job and the projects we're working on, but I've also been pursuing some personal interests in writing and painting. I'm wondering if we could discuss the possibility of adjusting my responsibilities to allow for a more flexible schedule."

Greg listened intently as Clara laid out her thoughts. To her surprise, he nodded thoughtfully. "I appreciate your honesty, Clara. It's great to hear you're pursuing your passions. Why don't we look at your current projects and see where we can create some flexibility? I want you to feel fulfilled in both your work and your personal life."

The relief that washed over Clara was palpable. The conversation with Greg opened up new possibilities, allowing her to envision a future where she could balance her corporate career and her creative pursuits. They spent the next hour discussing her workload, ultimately agreeing on a plan that would provide her with a couple of extra hours each week to dedicate to her writing and painting.

With her schedule adjusted, Clara felt an invigorating sense of freedom. She dove into her creative work with renewed vigor. The art exhibit was just a few weeks away, and Clara was eager to showcase her pieces. Her nights became filled with painting sessions, often accompanied by soft music and steaming cups of herbal tea. The colors she mixed on her palette danced in harmony, mirroring the excitement blooming in her heart.

In her writing class, Clara began to explore deeper themes—identity, transition, and the pursuit of passion. Mr. Carter encouraged her to tap into her own experiences, to write what she knew, and her pieces began to take on a more personal tone. She wrote about her fears, her aspirations, and the challenges of starting anew in her late forties.

One evening, Clara wrote a short story titled "The Second Bloom," which was about a woman who rediscovered her love for painting after years of putting her dreams aside. The protagonist faced obstacles but ultimately learned to embrace her art as a vital part of her identity. As she typed the final words, Clara felt tears of joy welling up in her eyes. It was as if she had written her own journey, a reflection of the struggles and triumphs she experienced.

As the day of the art exhibit approached, Clara felt a mixture of excitement and nerves. She spent hours preparing her pieces, ensuring that each painting was framed beautifully and ready for display. The thought of showcasing her work to the public filled her with anticipation, but also with self-doubt. What if people didn't connect with her art? What if they didn't see the beauty in her journey?

On the day of the exhibit, Clara arrived at the community center early to set up her work. She arranged the paintings carefully, stepping back occasionally to assess the overall composition of the display. As she hung the last piece, an abstract painting symbolizing her journey of transformation, she took a deep breath, allowing herself to soak in the moment. This was it—the culmination of her hard work and dedication.

As the evening began, guests flowed into the center, mingling and admiring the artwork on display. Clara found herself chatting with visitors, sharing her story and the inspiration behind each piece. The warm glow of the lights and the sound of laughter filled the air, creating an atmosphere of celebration.

Clara felt a sense of camaraderie with the other artists, who were equally passionate about their work. They exchanged ideas, critiques, and encouragement, creating a community that felt supportive and invigorating. In those moments, Clara realized that she was not alone on this journey—others were navigating their paths too.

As the night wore on, Clara received positive feedback about her paintings. Guests praised her use of color and the emotional depth of her work. Each compliment reinforced her belief that she was on the right path. She connected with people who shared similar experiences, and the conversations flowed effortlessly. Clara felt a surge of confidence; the fear that had lingered in her heart began to dissipate.

At the end of the evening, as guests filtered out, Clara took a moment to reflect on the night. She stood before her artwork, feeling a profound sense of accomplishment. This exhibit was not just a showcase of her talent; it was a celebration of her journey, her resilience, and her refusal to give up on her dreams.

That night, Clara returned home with her heart full and her spirit soaring. The challenges she had faced were merely stepping stones toward her aspirations. As she drifted off to sleep, she felt a sense of peace enveloping her, knowing that she was embracing the challenges of life with courage and determination. Clara had stepped into a new chapter of her life, and the story was only just beginning.

5

New Connections

In the weeks following the art exhibit, Clara felt a renewed sense of purpose. The success of her first show invigorated her, and she was eager to embrace new experiences. Encouraged by the positive feedback she received, Clara signed up for several local art workshops and writing groups, seeking to expand her skills and meet like-minded individuals.

One crisp Saturday morning, Clara attended a watercolor workshop at a nearby community center. The bright studio, filled with natural light streaming through large windows, buzzed with excitement as participants gathered. Clara felt a mix of nervousness and anticipation. Although she had begun to find her footing in the artistic community, stepping into a new environment still brought with it a familiar wave of insecurity.

As Clara took her seat at a table, she noticed a woman across from her with vibrant blue hair and a welcoming smile. "Hi there! I'm Jess," the woman introduced herself, her enthusiasm infectious. "Are you new to watercolor?"

"Hi, I'm Clara. Yes, this is my first workshop," she replied, feeling instantly at ease.

"Great! I've been painting for years, but I'm always learning something new.

You'll love it here," Jess assured her, and Clara felt a flicker of excitement at the prospect of honing her craft alongside someone so passionate.

The workshop began with the instructor demonstrating various techniques. Clara watched intently as he mixed colors on his palette, fascinated by the way the paint flowed across the paper. With each stroke, Clara felt her inhibitions begin to fade. She picked up her brush and tried her hand at the techniques demonstrated, slowly allowing her creativity to take shape.

Throughout the session, Clara and Jess struck up a conversation that flowed effortlessly. They shared their backgrounds, dreams, and the challenges they faced as artists. Jess spoke about her journey as a musician turned visual artist, explaining how she used her art to express the emotions she felt through her music. Clara was captivated by her passion and authenticity.

After the workshop, the two women exchanged contact information, excited to keep in touch. Clara left the studio feeling buoyant. The experience had reignited her love for painting, and she was eager to explore this newfound friendship.

Over the next few weeks, Clara and Jess met regularly. They visited local galleries, explored art supply stores, and even joined a weekend sketching group in the park. Each encounter deepened their bond, and Clara found herself opening up in ways she hadn't anticipated. Sharing her aspirations and fears with Jess felt liberating; it was a reminder that she was not alone on her journey.

One evening, while they were sitting on a bench overlooking the river, Jess turned to Clara, a contemplative look in her eyes. "You know, I used to be terrified of putting my music out there. I worried no one would understand it or like it. But I learned that creating is about expressing yourself, not seeking validation from others."

Clara nodded, understanding all too well the fear that accompanied sharing one's art. "I feel the same way. I constantly battle the thought that maybe I'm not good enough. But I want to push through that fear."

"Exactly! Let's challenge ourselves," Jess proposed, her excitement palpable. "How about we create a piece together for a local art fair? We could combine your painting skills and my music. We can make something truly unique!"

The idea sparked a fire in Clara's heart. "That sounds incredible! I'd love to!" she exclaimed, feeling a wave of inspiration wash over her.

As they began to plan their collaborative piece, Clara felt a renewed sense of creativity blooming within her. They decided to create a multimedia artwork that blended watercolor with musical elements—something that reflected both of their artistic journeys. Clara would paint vibrant landscapes, while Jess would compose a short melody to accompany the visuals.

The project brought them even closer, as they spent hours brainstorming ideas, sketching, and experimenting with their respective mediums. Clara found herself losing track of time in the studio, reveling in the joy of creation. The process was both challenging and exhilarating, as they navigated each other's strengths and weaknesses, encouraging one another to step out of their comfort zones.

As the art fair approached, Clara felt a mix of anticipation and anxiety. She had never collaborated on a project before, let alone one that involved sharing her work with the public. The thought of presenting their piece to an audience filled her with both excitement and dread.

On the day of the fair, Clara and Jess arrived early to set up their display. Clara's heart raced as they arranged their artwork, a large canvas painted with sweeping strokes of blue and green, reminiscent of a serene landscape. Beside it, a small speaker was set up to play Jess's melodic composition, which they had synchronized perfectly with the visual presentation.

As the fair opened, visitors began to flow through the booths. Clara felt a mixture of pride and vulnerability as she watched people engage with their work. Some stopped to listen to Jess's melody while admiring the painting, and Clara overheard snippets of conversation, filled with praise and intrigue.

When it was time for their presentation, Clara took a deep breath. Standing next to Jess, she felt an overwhelming sense of gratitude for their partnership. As they spoke about their project and the inspiration behind it, Clara realized that sharing her art was not just about showcasing her talent—it was about connecting with others and celebrating the beauty of collaboration.

The experience was transformative for Clara. She felt empowered by the encouragement from her peers and the warmth of the community surrounding her. She had taken significant steps outside her comfort zone, embracing her fears and pursuing her passions wholeheartedly. The connections she had forged with Jess and the art community had not only enriched her artistic journey but also deepened her understanding of the importance of relationships in the pursuit of dreams.

That night, as Clara returned home, she reflected on how far she had come. The hurdles she had faced were now stepping stones in her journey, leading her to a place of creativity, connection, and self-discovery. She was excited about what lay ahead, ready to embrace the challenges and opportunities that awaited her in this new chapter of her life.

6

The Art of Letting Go

As summer transitioned into fall, Clara found herself reflecting on the changes in her life. The vibrant colors of the leaves mirrored her own transformation; she felt alive with creativity and connection. However, beneath the surface of her newfound joy lay an unsettling undercurrent: the anxiety of balancing her burgeoning artistic career with her responsibilities at home.

After her successful collaboration with Jess, Clara began receiving invitations to participate in more exhibits and workshops. While she was thrilled at the opportunities, her calendar quickly filled with commitments, and the pressure began to mount. Balancing her artistic pursuits with her family responsibilities proved to be a daunting challenge.

One evening, after a long day of painting, Clara sat at her kitchen table surrounded by sketches and art supplies. She glanced at the clock; it was nearly 8 p.m., and she hadn't yet prepared dinner for her family. Guilt washed over her. She had always prided herself on being a dedicated mother and wife, but lately, she felt like she was failing in both roles.

Her husband, Mark, entered the kitchen with a weary smile. "Hey, Clara, I ordered pizza. You've been working so hard," he said, sensing her tension.

"Thanks, Mark," she replied, grateful but still weighed down by her unfinished tasks. "I'm sorry I didn't have time to cook. I've just been so busy with my art."

"It's okay," he reassured her. "I love seeing you pursue your passion, but you need to take care of yourself too. You can't pour from an empty cup."

Clara sighed, feeling torn between her responsibilities and her desire to create. "I know, but I'm afraid if I slow down, I'll lose the momentum I've built. What if I miss out on opportunities?"

Mark took a seat across from her, resting his elbows on the table. "You won't lose anything by taking a break. Sometimes stepping back is what we need to see things more clearly. Remember that you're not alone in this; we're a team."

His words lingered in her mind long after their conversation ended. Clara realized she had been so focused on her artistic growth that she had neglected her well-being and the needs of her family. She was so eager to prove herself in her new career that she had forgotten the importance of balance.

That night, Clara decided to take Mark's advice to heart. The next day, she began clearing her schedule, consciously choosing to prioritize quality time with her family. She canceled a few art commitments, much to her surprise, and planned a weekend getaway to a nearby cabin with Mark and their kids, Emma and Noah.

As they arrived at the cozy cabin, nestled among towering trees and vibrant foliage, Clara felt a sense of relief wash over her. The scent of pine and crisp autumn air invigorated her spirit. The family settled in, and Clara took a moment to soak in the beauty surrounding them.

That evening, they gathered around a crackling fire outside, roasting marshmallows and sharing stories. Clara found herself laughing more freely than she had in weeks. She realized how much she had missed these simple moments of connection with her family. Emma and Noah's laughter filled the air, and for the first time in a long while, Clara felt the weight on her shoulders begin to lift.

As the sun dipped below the horizon, Clara pulled out her sketchbook, inspired by the beauty of the natural world around her. The soft glow of the firelight illuminated the pages as she began to sketch the outline of the trees against the dusky sky. With each stroke of her pencil, she felt a sense of liberation. The pressure to produce art for exhibits faded, replaced by the pure joy of creation.

"Can I draw with you?" Emma asked, her eyes sparkling with curiosity.

"Of course! I'd love that," Clara replied, smiling as she handed her daughter a spare pencil.

As they sat side by side, Clara guided Emma in sketching the trees, encouraging her to embrace her own artistic instincts. She felt a sense of fulfillment in sharing this moment with her daughter, realizing that creativity was not just about individual expression but also about connecting with others.

Later that night, as Clara lay in bed, she reflected on the day. The retreat had reminded her of what truly mattered—her family, their shared moments, and the importance of nurturing relationships. She understood now that she didn't have to sacrifice one passion for another. Instead, she could find a way to integrate her love for art into her family life.

The next week, with her family firmly in her heart, Clara returned home with a renewed sense of clarity. She decided to create a new routine that would allow her to devote time to her art while still being present for her family. Clara began scheduling dedicated time for painting and sketching, while also committing to family activities, ensuring that both her artistic pursuits and family life received the attention they deserved.

With each passing week, Clara found a rhythm that worked for her. She began to invite her family into her creative process. Emma and Noah became her enthusiastic little helpers, participating in art sessions where they would paint together, each creating their own masterpieces. Clara cherished these moments, as they turned into family bonding experiences filled with laughter and creativity.

As autumn progressed and the leaves began to fall, Clara felt a sense of fulfillment she hadn't experienced before. She was no longer just Clara, the artist; she was also Clara, the mother, the wife, and the creator. This newfound understanding allowed her to let go of the unrealistic expectations she had placed upon herself. Instead of viewing her art career as something separate from her family life, she embraced it as a part of the beautiful tapestry they were weaving together.

Clara realized that creativity thrived in an environment of love and support. By nurturing her relationships, she not only enriched her art but also cultivated a deeper connection with her family. In letting go of the pressure to achieve success on her own terms, she found a path to fulfillment that resonated with her heart.

As winter approached, Clara prepared for her next exhibit, feeling ready to share her work once again. But this time, she carried with her the lessons she had learned about balance, connection, and the art of letting go.

7

Embracing Vulnerability

The winter chill settled over the town, blanketing everything in a soft layer of snow. Clara welcomed the quiet beauty of the season, finding solace in the stillness that surrounded her. As the holidays approached, she reflected on the past few months and the profound changes in her life. She felt stronger, more grounded, and ready to embrace the challenges ahead.

With her upcoming exhibit just weeks away, Clara was busy preparing her pieces. She had decided to showcase a series of paintings inspired by her family and the love that flowed through their lives. Each canvas captured a moment of joy: Emma and Noah laughing in the park, Mark cooking dinner while Clara painted in the background, and family game nights that filled their home with warmth and laughter. The paintings were vibrant, full of color and life—expressions of her heart and the moments she held dear.

However, as Clara immersed herself in her work, doubt began to creep in. Would people connect with these personal pieces? Would they understand the depth of her emotions? The fear of vulnerability washed over her, threatening to overshadow the joy of creation. Clara had always been hesitant to expose her inner feelings through her art, fearing judgment or misunderstanding. But she knew that her journey had taught her the value of authenticity, and perhaps this was the moment to fully embrace that lesson.

One evening, Clara invited Jess over for a final review of her work before the exhibit. As the two women sipped hot cocoa in the cozy warmth of Clara's living room, Clara unveiled the series of paintings, her heart pounding in her chest.

"Wow, Clara! These are beautiful!" Jess exclaimed, her eyes sparkling with enthusiasm. "The colors, the emotions—it's all so vibrant and alive."

"Thanks, Jess," Clara replied, feeling a mix of pride and anxiety. "But I'm nervous. I've always painted from a place of observation, not personal experience. What if people think it's too sentimental?"

"Art is meant to evoke emotions," Jess said, leaning in closer. "Your experiences, your family, those are the things that make your art unique. You have a voice, and it's powerful. Don't shy away from it."

Clara took a deep breath, trying to absorb Jess's words. "You're right. I want my art to resonate with others, but I'm afraid of being too exposed."

"Vulnerability is a strength, not a weakness," Jess encouraged. "By sharing your true self, you invite others to connect with you. It's scary, but it's also incredibly liberating. You have to trust that the right people will appreciate your honesty."

That night, as Clara lay in bed, Jess's words replayed in her mind. She realized that her journey was about more than just creating art; it was about embracing her vulnerability and allowing others to see her true self. Clara knew she had to let go of her fears and trust in the beauty of her experiences.

As the day of the exhibit approached, Clara poured herself into her work, her passion igniting with each brushstroke. She added the finishing touches to her paintings, infusing them with emotion and depth. Each piece was a reflection of her heart, a celebration of the love she shared with her family.

On the night of the exhibit, Clara felt a whirlwind of emotions—excitement, anxiety, and a tinge of fear. The gallery buzzed with energy as artists, friends, and family gathered to admire the work on display. Clara arrived early, her heart racing as she set up her pieces, the vibrant colors of her paintings popping against the stark white walls.

As the doors opened, Clara welcomed guests with a smile, though her stomach churned with nerves. She watched as people moved through the gallery, admiring the artwork. Some lingered before her pieces, whispering to one another, and Clara's heart swelled with both pride and apprehension.

Then, a moment came that would change everything. An older woman approached Clara, her eyes brimming with tears. "This painting," she said, pointing to a piece that depicted a family playing in the park, "it reminds me of my own grandchildren. It brings back such happy memories. Thank you for capturing that feeling."

Clara's heart swelled. "I'm so glad it resonates with you," she replied, feeling a deep connection to this stranger who understood her art on a personal level.

As the evening continued, more guests shared their thoughts on Clara's work. Each comment, each story, was a reminder that her vulnerability had opened a door to connection. People were responding to the emotions she had poured into her art, and the fear that had once held her back began to dissipate.

Throughout the night, Clara engaged with her guests, sharing stories behind each piece. She spoke of her family, her creative process, and the importance of love and connection in her life. As she shared her heart, she felt an incredible sense of liberation. The act of being vulnerable allowed others to feel seen and understood, creating a space for meaningful conversations and connections.

Toward the end of the evening, Jess found Clara standing in front of her favorite painting—a portrait of her family gathered around the dinner table, laughter captured in a moment of joy. "You did it, Clara," Jess said, beaming with pride. "You embraced vulnerability, and look at the impact it's had."

Clara smiled, her heart full. "I didn't realize how much I needed this. It feels incredible to share my story through my art."

The exhibit proved to be a turning point for Clara. In embracing her vulnerability, she discovered not only her artistic voice but also the power of connection. The experience taught her that sharing her truth could resonate with others in profound ways, igniting conversations and fostering understanding.

As the night drew to a close, Clara felt a deep sense of gratitude. She had taken a leap of faith, and it had led her to a place of acceptance and self-discovery. The journey of embracing vulnerability would continue, but Clara was ready to navigate whatever lay ahead, armed with the knowledge that her art could bridge the gap between hearts, forging connections that transcended fear.

With the exhibit behind her, Clara looked forward to new opportunities. She knew that being vulnerable would remain a challenge, but it was a challenge she was willing to embrace. After all, vulnerability was not a weakness; it was a testament to her courage and the beautiful complexity of being human.

8

A New Chapter Begins

As winter deepened and the snow piled high outside, Clara felt a surge of energy and possibility within her. The success of her exhibit had ignited a fire in her that she had never experienced before. Encouraged by the positive reception of her work and the connections she had made, Clara began to dream bigger.

She had always painted for herself and her family, but now she wanted to share her art with a broader audience. Clara envisioned herself hosting workshops, teaching others to connect with their emotions through art. The idea thrilled her, but it also filled her with apprehension. What if she wasn't good enough? What if she failed?

One evening, as she sat with Mark, sharing her ideas over dinner, Clara found the courage to voice her dreams. "Mark, I've been thinking about hosting some art workshops. I want to teach others how to express themselves through painting," she said, her voice trembling slightly.

Mark looked up, intrigued. "That sounds amazing! You have so much to offer, Clara. I think it could be a wonderful experience for you and for others."

"I want to create a space where people can feel safe to explore their creativity, just like I did," Clara continued, her passion bubbling over. "But what if nobody shows up? What if I'm not a good teacher?"

"Clara, you can't let fear hold you back," Mark encouraged, reaching across the table to squeeze her hand. "You've come so far, and you have so much to share. Remember the first time you showed your art? Look at how you've grown since then. Just take it one step at a time."

His words resonated with her. Clara knew that stepping into this new role would require her to lean into her vulnerability, but she felt ready to embrace the challenge. Inspired by Mark's support, she decided to move forward with her plans.

Over the next few weeks, Clara dedicated her evenings to organizing her first workshop. She envisioned a cozy space filled with light, laughter, and creativity. After securing a local community center for the event, she created flyers, promoted the workshop on social media, and reached out to her network. With each passing day, the excitement mixed with nerves continued to build.

Finally, the day of the workshop arrived. Clara arrived early, setting up the space with paints, brushes, and canvases. She filled the room with colorful decorations and played soft music in the background. As she prepared, Clara couldn't help but feel a wave of anxiety wash over her. What if no one came? What if she couldn't teach effectively?

As participants began to trickle in, Clara's heart raced. They ranged in age and backgrounds, each with their own stories and experiences. Some were seasoned artists looking to explore a new medium, while others were complete beginners seeking an outlet for their emotions. Clara felt an immediate connection with each one, recognizing their shared desire to create.

"Welcome, everyone!" Clara said, her voice warm and inviting. "I'm so glad you're here today. My goal is to create a space where you can explore your creativity and express yourselves freely. There's no right or wrong in art, just your unique expression."

As she guided the group through warm-up exercises and painting techniques, Clara felt her initial nerves fade. She shared stories of her own journey, encouraging participants to let go of self-doubt and embrace their creativity. The energy in the room was electric as people picked up their brushes and began to create.

Clara moved among the tables, offering support and encouragement. She witnessed the joy on their faces as they explored colors and forms, often losing themselves in the process. She remembered her own experience of liberation while painting, and it filled her with a sense of fulfillment to see others experiencing the same joy.

One participant, an older woman named Miriam, approached Clara with a canvas filled with bold, swirling colors. "I haven't painted in years," she admitted, her voice trembling with emotion. "But today, I felt like I could let go of everything and just create."

Clara smiled, her heart swelling with pride. "That's the beauty of art—it allows us to express what we sometimes can't put into words. You've done an incredible job!"

As the workshop progressed, Clara's confidence blossomed. The room buzzed with laughter, creativity, and connection. She encouraged her participants to share their stories, and in turn, they opened up about their lives—their struggles, their joys, and the healing power of art. Clara felt a profound sense of belonging as she realized they were all in this together, united by a shared passion for creativity.

As the workshop came to a close, Clara gathered everyone together to share their work. Each person proudly displayed their paintings, and Clara marveled at the diversity of expression in the room. The smiles on their faces and the sense of community warmed her heart.

"Thank you all for being a part of this experience," Clara said, her voice filled with emotion. "You've reminded me of the power of vulnerability and connection through art. I hope you continue to explore your creativity and share your stories with the world."

After the participants left, Clara sat in the now-quiet room, overwhelmed with gratitude. She had faced her fears and stepped into a new role, and the experience had changed her in ways she hadn't anticipated. The workshop had not only allowed her to share her passion but also helped her discover a deeper purpose in her art.

That evening, as Clara returned home, Mark greeted her with open arms. "How did it go?" he asked, excitement sparkling in his eyes.

"It was amazing, Mark! I can't believe how much joy it brought me and everyone else. I want to do this again!" Clara exclaimed, her enthusiasm bubbling over.

Mark smiled, pride shining in his eyes. "I knew you'd be great at it. You have a gift for bringing people together and helping them see the beauty in themselves."

As Clara settled into bed that night, her heart was full. She had embraced vulnerability, shared her passion, and connected with others on a profound level. This was only the beginning of her journey, and she felt more committed than ever to nurturing her new path as an artist and a teacher.

In the weeks that followed, Clara continued to host workshops, each one filling her with excitement and purpose. She discovered the power of community and the impact art could have on people's lives. Each participant's journey enriched her own, and she felt a renewed sense of belonging.

Clara's art transformed from a solitary pursuit into a shared experience, bringing joy to not just her own life but also the lives of those around her. As she continued to embrace vulnerability, she realized that this was not just about her career shift; it was about creating a legacy of connection, creativity, and love.

With each new workshop, Clara felt her own artistic spirit grow stronger, and she couldn't wait to see what adventures awaited her on this new chapter of her life.

9

Embracing Challenges

As spring arrived, bringing with it the scent of blooming flowers and the warmth of the sun, Clara found herself at a pivotal moment in her newfound career. The success of her workshops had attracted attention beyond her expectations, and she was approached by a local art gallery interested in showcasing her work. It was a dream opportunity, yet it also filled her with a sense of apprehension. What if she failed to meet their expectations?

The gallery director, a charismatic woman named Lydia, had attended one of Clara's workshops and was captivated by the authenticity and emotion in her paintings. During their meeting, Lydia expressed her admiration for Clara's unique style and encouraged her to submit a collection for an upcoming group exhibition themed "Resilience and Renewal."

Clara sat across from Lydia in the cozy café where they had met, her hands trembling slightly around her cup of tea. "Thank you for believing in me," Clara said, her voice barely above a whisper. "But I'm not sure I'm ready for an exhibition. What if my work isn't good enough?"

"Clara, you have a gift," Lydia replied, her eyes sparkling with enthusiasm. "You've already connected with so many people through your art. This exhibition could be a wonderful opportunity for you to share your journey.

You owe it to yourself to take this chance."

Clara felt a mixture of excitement and fear. She had never envisioned herself exhibiting in a gallery, yet the thought of sharing her art with a broader audience ignited something within her. After much contemplation, she decided to accept the challenge. It was time to push her boundaries and embrace the possibility of growth.

Over the next few weeks, Clara threw herself into her work with renewed vigor. She spent countless hours in her studio, experimenting with colors, techniques, and themes that spoke to her experience of resilience and transformation. She poured her heart into each piece, reflecting on her journey of self-discovery and the power of art as a medium for healing.

However, as the deadline for submission approached, Clara began to feel overwhelmed. Doubts crept in like unwelcome shadows, and she found herself questioning her abilities. "What if I'm just a fraud?" she mused to Mark one evening as they prepared dinner together. "What if they see my work and realize I'm not an artist, just a woman playing dress-up?"

Mark paused, turning to her with a look of concern. "Clara, you're not a fraud. You've put in the hard work, and your art speaks for itself. Remember what you told your workshop participants? It's about the process, not just the end result. You've already inspired so many people."

His words offered her a glimmer of hope, and she decided to focus on the joy of creating rather than the fear of judgment. Clara poured herself into her work, exploring deeper themes of resilience—how life's challenges had shaped her, and how her art had become a sanctuary for her emotions.

On the day of submission, Clara stood in front of her finished pieces, each canvas a reflection of her journey. She felt a wave of pride wash over her as she loaded her paintings into the car, ready to deliver them to the gallery. As she drove, her heart raced with excitement and fear.

Upon arriving at the gallery, Clara was greeted warmly by Lydia and the gallery staff. They helped her unload the paintings, offering compliments that eased some of Clara's anxiety. "These are stunning, Clara. I can't wait for everyone to see them!" Lydia exclaimed as she examined each piece.

Despite the support, Clara still felt a flutter of unease in her stomach. Would her work resonate with others? Would they see the depth of emotion she had poured into each brushstroke?

After submitting her pieces, Clara left the gallery feeling a mixture of exhilaration and vulnerability. She had stepped into the unknown and taken a significant leap of faith, and she felt both proud and terrified.

In the days that followed, Clara focused on preparing for the exhibition opening. She organized her next round of workshops, hoping to share the news of her upcoming show with her students. During one session, she decided to share her experience with the gallery submission process, using it as a teaching moment.

"I want you all to know that fear is a part of the journey," Clara began, addressing her participants. "I was scared to submit my work for an exhibition, but I chose to embrace that fear and take a leap of faith. It's not about being perfect; it's about expressing yourself and allowing your art to speak."

The participants listened intently, some nodding in understanding. Clara could see the inspiration growing in their eyes, and she felt a renewed sense of purpose. Her journey was not just about her own growth but about encouraging others to pursue their passions, no matter how daunting they may seem.

As the opening night of the exhibition approached, Clara found herself in a whirlwind of emotions. She was excited to showcase her work but also fearful of the reception it would receive. The day before the exhibition, Clara decided to revisit the gallery for a final walkthrough.

Walking through the space, Clara admired how the lighting highlighted her paintings. Each piece resonated with the theme of resilience, and she felt a deep sense of connection to her work. Clara paused in front of her favorite piece, a vibrant abstract painting that symbolized her transformation from self-doubt to self-acceptance.

Suddenly, a wave of emotions washed over her—pride, gratitude, and a hint of disbelief. Clara took a deep breath, reminding herself of the journey that had brought her to this moment. She had transformed her fears into fuel for creativity, and regardless of the outcome, she was proud of what she had accomplished.

The opening night arrived, and Clara donned her favorite dress, a flowing garment that made her feel both comfortable and confident. As she entered the gallery, she was struck by the number of people milling about, admiring the art. Lydia greeted her with a warm hug, and Clara felt a sense of belonging in the bustling atmosphere.

Throughout the evening, Clara mingled with fellow artists, art enthusiasts, and friends. She was overwhelmed by the positive feedback on her work. People resonated with the themes of resilience and transformation, sharing their own stories of struggle and triumph. Clara found herself engaged in heartfelt conversations that reminded her of the power of connection through art.

As the night drew to a close, Clara stood before her favorite piece, surrounded by a small group of admirers. They expressed how her work had inspired them to reflect on their own journeys. Clara felt a wave of emotion as she realized that she had not only shared her art but also created a space for others to explore their own resilience.

That night, as she returned home, Clara reflected on the transformative power of vulnerability. She had faced her fears, embraced challenges, and created art that resonated with others. In doing so, she had discovered a profound sense of purpose and belonging in her new career.

Clara knew that this was just the beginning of her journey. She was committed to continuing to embrace the challenges ahead, knowing that each step would only deepen her connection to herself and her art. As she drifted off to sleep, she felt a renewed sense of hope and excitement for what lay ahead in her life—a life transformed by creativity, resilience, and the courage to embrace change.

10

A New Direction

As the exhibition came to a close, Clara felt a mixture of satisfaction and uncertainty. The event had been a resounding success; her paintings had sparked conversations, and she received offers for commissions and future workshops. Yet, amid this triumph, she sensed a yearning for something more—a desire to expand her artistic journey beyond what she had initially envisioned.

In the weeks following the exhibition, Clara took the time to reflect on her experiences. The joy she felt from creating and sharing her art was undeniable, but she began to wonder if there was a way to merge her passion for art with her desire to make a difference in the community. She thought back to her early career in social work, where she had helped individuals navigate their challenges, and a new idea began to form.

One afternoon, while sipping tea in her sunlit kitchen, Clara picked up her notebook and began jotting down her thoughts. "Art therapy," she wrote at the top of the page. The concept had always fascinated her—the idea of using art as a therapeutic tool to help individuals express their emotions and heal from trauma. She had seen firsthand how powerful creativity could be in her own life, and now she envisioned a program where she could blend her love for painting with her passion for helping others.

With newfound determination, Clara researched art therapy programs and the requirements to become certified. She discovered that many organizations offered courses and workshops for aspiring art therapists. The idea of returning to school filled her with excitement but also apprehension. Would she be able to manage another round of education alongside her painting and workshops?

Despite her doubts, Clara decided to take the plunge. She enrolled in an online course that focused on art therapy principles and practices, knowing that it would equip her with the skills to facilitate healing through art. As she began her studies, Clara felt a renewed sense of purpose. Each lesson reignited her passion for creativity, and she eagerly absorbed the knowledge, excited to explore how art could impact mental health and well-being.

Around this time, Clara also connected with a local community center that was looking for innovative ways to engage residents. After meeting with the director, she proposed the idea of starting an art therapy program aimed at helping individuals dealing with anxiety, depression, and other emotional challenges. The director was enthusiastic about the concept, recognizing the need for mental health resources in the community.

"Your passion for art and helping others is exactly what we need," he said, his eyes lighting up. "Let's work together to make this happen."

Clara's heart soared at the prospect of bringing her vision to life. Over the next few weeks, she collaborated with the community center to develop a curriculum that integrated art activities with discussions about emotional well-being. They planned weekly sessions that would provide a safe space for participants to express themselves through various art forms, from painting and drawing to collage and sculpture.

As Clara prepared for the first session, she felt a blend of excitement and nerves. She had led art workshops before, but this was different; it felt more personal and impactful. The night before the first class, she stayed up late, double-checking her materials and crafting an outline for the session. She wanted to ensure that participants would feel welcomed and encouraged to express their emotions.

On the day of the first session, Clara arrived early to set up the room. She arranged tables covered in art supplies, from paints and brushes to clay and markers. As participants began to arrive, she greeted them with warm smiles and open arms. Some looked apprehensive, while others seemed eager to dive into the creative process.

"Welcome, everyone! I'm so glad you're here," Clara said, her voice full of enthusiasm. "Today, we're going to explore our feelings through art. There's no right or wrong way to express yourself; this is all about you and what you want to create."

As the session unfolded, Clara guided the group through various exercises, encouraging them to embrace their emotions and let their creativity flow. She introduced a theme of "expressing joy," inviting participants to paint or draw moments in their lives that brought them happiness.

At first, some participants hesitated, unsure of what to create. Clara shared her own story of struggle and the ways art had helped her navigate difficult times. Slowly but surely, participants began to pick up brushes and pens, their initial apprehension melting away as they immersed themselves in their work.

Clara moved around the room, offering support and encouragement. She was struck by the profound transformation happening before her eyes. Participants who had come in feeling reserved and anxious began to share their stories as they painted. Laughter and tears filled the space as they connected through their art.

One participant, a middle-aged woman named Sarah, opened up about her recent struggles with grief after losing her mother. "I didn't know how to express this pain," she admitted, her eyes glistening with unshed tears. "But painting this memory of her is helping me process it."

Clara's heart swelled with empathy. "Thank you for sharing that, Sarah. It's powerful to honor those we've lost through our art. You're not alone in this journey."

As the session came to a close, Clara felt a deep sense of fulfillment. The participants had created beautiful pieces that reflected their emotions, and the room buzzed with a newfound sense of community. Clara knew that this was only the beginning of a transformative journey for everyone involved.

In the weeks that followed, Clara's art therapy program gained momentum. Participants began to return regularly, and word spread throughout the community about the healing power of art. Clara witnessed firsthand how creativity could facilitate conversations about mental health, allowing individuals to confront their emotions in a safe and supportive environment.

One evening, as Clara cleaned up after a session, she received an unexpected message from Lydia. The gallery director wanted to meet and discuss an opportunity that could further elevate Clara's work. Intrigued and a bit nervous, Clara agreed to meet Lydia at the café where they had first connected.

When they met, Lydia shared her vision for a community art initiative that would focus on mental health awareness. "I believe your art therapy program aligns perfectly with this project," she explained. "We're planning a collaborative exhibition that features art created by individuals in therapy programs, highlighting their journeys and the impact of creativity on mental health."

Clara's heart raced with excitement. This was an incredible opportunity to showcase not only her work but also the collective experiences of those participating in her program. She felt a surge of inspiration as she envisioned the powerful stories that could be told through art.

"I would love to be a part of this," Clara said, her voice filled with enthusiasm. "It's a chance to amplify the voices of those who are often unheard and to emphasize the importance of mental health."

As they discussed the details, Clara felt a renewed sense of purpose. She was not only creating art for herself but also facilitating healing for others, and now she had the opportunity to share their stories with a wider audience.

That night, Clara returned home feeling invigorated and hopeful. Her career shift had led her to a path she never imagined, one filled with creativity, connection, and purpose. With each brushstroke and each session, she was not only transforming her life but also touching the lives of others in profound ways.

The journey was far from over, but Clara was ready to embrace the next chapter with open arms, knowing that she was on a path that blended her passions for art and helping others in a meaningful way. The future looked bright, and Clara was excited to see where this new direction would lead her.

11

The Collective Exhibition

As the day of the exhibition approached, Clara felt a mix of anticipation and nervousness. The collaborative art show was not just about her paintings; it was about the collective stories and experiences of the participants in her art therapy program. She had spent countless hours helping others express their emotions through art, and now, their creations would be displayed for the community to see. It was a significant moment that could raise awareness about mental health and the healing power of creativity.

In the weeks leading up to the exhibition, Clara worked tirelessly alongside Lydia and the community center staff to coordinate the event. They set a date and secured a local gallery for the show, which they named "Voices of Healing." Each participant from Clara's program was invited to contribute their artwork, and Clara encouraged them to share the stories behind their pieces.

On the night of the exhibition, Clara arrived early to help set up the gallery. The atmosphere was electric as she and the volunteers hung the artwork, carefully curating the layout to create a flow that would guide visitors through the stories being told. Clara felt a surge of pride as she saw the diversity of the artwork—paintings, drawings, and mixed-media pieces, each reflecting the unique journey of the artist.

As guests began to arrive, Clara mingled with the crowd, welcoming them with a warm smile. The gallery was filled with friends, family, and community members, all eager to support the artists. Clara took a moment to step back and observe the reactions of the attendees as they wandered through the gallery. Conversations flowed, and she could hear snippets of stories being shared about the pieces on the walls.

One of the most striking pieces was created by Sarah, the woman who had opened up about her grief during their first art therapy session. Her painting was a vibrant explosion of colors, depicting a garden filled with flowers that represented the memories of her mother. Clara watched as Sarah stood next to her artwork, nervously explaining its significance to a group of visitors. The way she spoke about her journey, from pain to healing, was inspiring.

"This garden represents the love and beauty my mother brought into my life," Sarah shared, her voice trembling but full of emotion. "Each flower symbolizes a cherished memory. Painting this helped me find peace amidst my grief."

Clara felt a rush of gratitude. This was the purpose of the exhibition—to provide a platform for people to share their stories and foster understanding around mental health issues. She could see the impact this experience was having on Sarah and the other participants, and it made all the hard work worth it.

As the evening progressed, Clara took a moment to step outside for some fresh air. The cool breeze brushed against her skin, and she took a deep breath, reflecting on the journey that had led her to this moment. She thought about her career shift, the doubts she had faced, and the risks she had taken. Each challenge had brought her closer to her true calling, and she felt a sense of fulfillment that she had never experienced before.

When she returned inside, she was greeted by Lydia, who had a big smile on her face. "Clara, this is incredible! The turnout is beyond what we expected, and the feedback on the artwork has been overwhelmingly positive. People are genuinely moved by the stories behind each piece."

Clara's heart swelled with joy at Lydia's words. They spent some time mingling with the guests, listening to their reactions and engaging in conversations about the art and the importance of mental health awareness. Clara realized that the exhibition was not only a celebration of creativity but also a vital step towards destigmatizing mental health struggles.

As the night began to wind down, Clara gathered the artists for a brief moment of reflection. "I just want to take a moment to acknowledge each of you," she said, her voice steady but filled with emotion. "You've shared your stories and your art with the community in such a powerful way. This exhibition is a testament to your strength and resilience. I'm so proud of each of you."

The artists exchanged smiles and nods, and Clara could see the pride radiating from their faces. They had created something beautiful together, and it was a reminder of the healing journey they were all on.

As the night drew to a close, Clara found herself reflecting on the impact of the exhibition. The event had sparked important conversations about mental health, encouraging attendees to share their experiences and support one another. Clara felt a sense of responsibility to continue this momentum and explore ways to integrate art therapy into more community initiatives.

In the following weeks, Clara began brainstorming ideas for future programs. She envisioned workshops focusing on specific themes, such as self-acceptance, resilience, and grief, allowing participants to delve deeper into their emotions. Clara also considered collaborating with local schools, introducing art therapy to students as a means of coping with academic pressures and social challenges.

With the success of the exhibition fresh in her mind, Clara felt invigorated by the possibilities ahead. The art therapy program had opened doors she never knew existed, and she was excited about the journey that lay ahead.

As she poured her heart into planning future sessions and workshops, Clara discovered a profound sense of purpose in her work. The collective exhibition had not only given her a platform to share her story but had also ignited a fire within her to advocate for mental health awareness and the healing power of art.

One evening, while working on her next set of lesson plans, Clara received an unexpected phone call from a local radio station. They had heard about the success of the exhibition and wanted to feature Clara and her program on their show, discussing the intersection of art and mental health. Clara's heart raced with excitement. This was an opportunity to reach even more people and share the importance of creativity in healing.

After hanging up the phone, Clara sat back in her chair, a smile spreading across her face. It felt as though the universe was aligning in her favor, guiding her towards a path filled with purpose and passion. The fear and uncertainty she had once felt about her career shift had transformed into confidence and clarity.

With renewed determination, Clara dived into her preparations for the radio interview, eager to share her journey and inspire others to explore the healing potential of art. She knew that her work was just beginning, and she was ready to embrace the challenges and opportunities that lay ahead.

The exhibition had marked a turning point in Clara's life, and she was excited to continue exploring the beautiful, intricate relationship between art, healing, and community. With each brushstroke, she felt empowered to make a difference, and she was committed to fostering a world where creativity could help heal hearts and minds.

12

New Beginnings

The morning sun poured through Clara's kitchen window, illuminating the small space filled with the vibrant colors of fresh fruit and the warm scent of brewed coffee. It was the day after the radio interview, and Clara still felt a rush of excitement as she recounted the experience to herself. The host had been genuinely interested in her work, asking insightful questions about her journey, the challenges she faced, and the impact of art therapy on mental health. Clara had shared not only her story but also the stories of her participants, who had bravely used their art to navigate through their personal struggles.

In the days following the interview, Clara noticed a shift in her life. The exposure had led to a surge of inquiries about her art therapy program. Local schools and community organizations were reaching out, eager to learn how they could incorporate art into their mental health initiatives. Clara felt overwhelmed but grateful for the opportunities that were unfolding before her.

With the increased interest in her program, Clara decided it was time to expand. She reached out to a few trusted colleagues in the field of mental health, inviting them to collaborate on a series of workshops that would reach different demographics within the community. Her vision was clear: to create a safe space for people of all ages to express their emotions through art while also providing them with tools to cope with life's challenges.

As Clara settled into her new routine, she began to develop a schedule for the workshops. Each session would focus on a specific theme, such as resilience, identity, or community. She was particularly excited about the idea of a summer program for teenagers, where they could explore their emotions and experiences through various art forms, including painting, sculpture, and digital media. Clara wanted to create an environment where they could not only learn about art but also connect with their peers and discuss the issues that mattered most to them.

Meanwhile, she continued to facilitate her regular art therapy sessions at the community center, where she saw familiar faces and new participants alike. Each session was filled with laughter, tears, and shared stories. Clara had created a beautiful tapestry of healing through art, where every individual's journey was honored and valued. The bonds that had formed among the participants became a source of strength and encouragement.

One day, as Clara was preparing for her upcoming workshop on resilience, she received a surprise visit from Sarah, the woman whose painting had touched so many during the exhibition. Sarah entered the community center with a bright smile, carrying a small canvas wrapped in colorful paper.

"Clara! I have something for you," she exclaimed, her eyes sparkling with excitement. "I wanted to thank you for everything you've done for me and for all of us in the program."

Clara's heart swelled with emotion as she unwrapped the canvas. It was a beautiful painting of a tree with deep roots and vibrant branches, symbolizing strength and growth. Below the tree, in delicate lettering, were the words, *"Rooted in Resilience."*

"Oh, Sarah! This is stunning!" Clara said, touched by the gesture. "You've captured the essence of our journey perfectly. Thank you so much!"

Sarah's cheeks flushed with pride. "I painted it as a reminder of how far we've all come. I want you to know that you've inspired me to keep going, to keep creating, and to keep sharing my story."

Clara felt tears prick at the corners of her eyes. This was the essence of why she had made her career shift. It was about the connections formed and the lives transformed through the power of art. As they stood together, admiring the painting, Clara knew that their shared journey was just beginning.

With the momentum from her recent successes, Clara took a leap of faith and applied for a grant to fund her expanded programs. The application process was rigorous, requiring detailed proposals and a clear vision for how the funding would benefit the community. Clara poured her heart into the application, weaving in the stories of her participants and the impact of art therapy on their lives.

Weeks passed, and the anticipation of the grant decision hung heavy in the air. Clara continued to stay busy with her workshops and sessions, but her mind often wandered back to the potential for expansion and how much more she could offer the community. She had faith in her mission and the belief that art could change lives.

Finally, the day arrived when she received the call from the grant committee. Clara held her breath as she answered, her heart racing. "Congratulations, Clara! We are thrilled to inform you that your proposal has been accepted. You will receive funding to implement your art therapy programs over the next year!"

The news was overwhelming. Clara felt a surge of joy and disbelief wash over her. She thanked the committee profusely, her heart swelling with gratitude and excitement. This was the breakthrough she had been hoping for—the opportunity to expand her reach, bring healing through art to more individuals, and ultimately make a lasting impact in her community.

With the funding secured, Clara set to work on implementing her vision. She reached out to schools, local nonprofits, and community centers to share her program. The response was overwhelmingly positive, and soon Clara found herself busy coordinating schedules and planning workshops for various age groups.

As the months passed, Clara watched her vision come to life. She led workshops filled with laughter and creativity, where participants explored their emotions, forged new friendships, and discovered the joy of expressing themselves through art. Each session was a reminder of the healing journey they were all on together.

Clara also started documenting the progress of her participants through photos and testimonials. She created a blog to share their stories, aiming to inspire others who might be struggling. Her website became a hub for mental health awareness and the transformative power of art, further establishing her as a voice in the community.

With each passing day, Clara felt more fulfilled and empowered. She had not only found a new career but had also discovered her purpose. The path she had taken, filled with uncertainty and doubt, had led her to a life rich with connection, creativity, and healing.

In her late 40s, Clara had embraced change and transformed her life in ways she had never imagined. She was no longer simply a woman shifting careers; she was a catalyst for change, an advocate for mental health, and a guide for those seeking solace through art. With her heart full and her spirit soaring, Clara knew that her journey was just beginning, and she was ready to embrace all the new beginnings that awaited her.

About the Author

Maryann is an author whose literary prowess knows no bounds. Hailing from a vibrant cultural background, she has a unique ability to weave together epic narratives that captivate readers and transport them into the heart of her stories. With a pen that dances across the pages, Maryann specializes in crafting tales that blend the realms of fiction with the nuances of real-life events, creating a rich tapestry of storytelling that resonates deeply with her audience.

From a young age, Maryann exhibited a profound love for literature. She would often be found nestled in a cozy corner of her local library, devouring books that spanned various genres. Inspired by the vivid characters and intricate plots she encountered, she began to dream of creating her own stories— tales that would inspire, provoke thought, and ignite the imagination. Her fascination with history and true events soon became a driving force in her writing, as she sought to explore the intricacies of the human experience through the lens of both fiction and reality.

Maryann's debut novel, Echoes of the future, established her as a formidable voice in contemporary literature. The book, which delves into the lives of individuals impacted by a significant historical event, received widespread acclaim for its immersive storytelling and well-researched background. Readers were drawn not only to the compelling characters but also to the authenticity of the events that shaped their lives. This blend of fact and fiction became a hallmark of Maryann's writing, captivating readers who craved stories that felt both real and extraordinary.

Her subsequent works continued to showcase her versatility as an author. In casting down, Maryann crafted a fantastical narrative steeped in cultural lore, exploring themes of destiny, love, and sacrifice. Through her vivid descriptions and emotional depth, she brought to life a world where mythical creatures and human struggles collided, captivating readers and leaving them longing for more. Each turn of the page revealed a layer of complexity, demonstrating her knack for weaving intricate plots that resonate long after the final chapter.

Beyond her novels, Maryann is also an advocate for aspiring writers. She often conducts workshops and writing retreats, sharing her knowledge and passion with those who dream of telling their own stories. Her commitment to nurturing new talent stems from her belief that everyone has a story worth telling. She encourages her students to embrace their unique voices and experiences, guiding them in discovering the power of storytelling as a means of connection and understanding.

Maryann Yinach's journey as an author is a testament to her unwavering dedication to the craft of writing. Her stories, whether drawn from the wellspring of her imagination or inspired by the truths of the world, resonate with a sense of epic scale and emotional depth. As she continues to explore the rich tapestry of human experiences through her writing, Maryann remains a beacon of inspiration for readers and writers alike, reminding us of the profound impact of a well-told story. With each new book, she invites us to embark on a journey of discovery, one that transcends the ordinary and celebrates the extraordinary in all its forms.

www.ingramcontent.com/pod-product-compliance
Lightning Source LLC
LaVergne TN
LVHW061603070526
838199LV00077B/7152